I0798838

Monsters, Zombies + Addicts

POEMS

Gwendolyn Zepeda

Monsters, Zombies + Addicts

POEMS

Gwendolyn Zepeda

Arte Público Press
Houston, Texas

Monsters, Zombies and Addicts is made possible through a grant from the City of Houston through the Houston Arts Alliance.

Recovering the past, creating the future

Arte Público Press
University of Houston
4902 Gulf Fwy, Rm 100
Houston, Texas 77204-2004

Cover design by Mora Des¡gn
Cover art by Alejandro Romero, "Atenea"

Zepeda, Gwendolyn.
[Poems. Selections]
Monsters, zombies and addicts : poems / by Gwendolyn Zepeda.
p cm
ISBN 978-1-55885-810-7 (softcover : acid-free paper)
I. Title.
PS3626.E46A6 2015
811'.6—dc23

2015003061
CIP

∞ The paper used in this publication meets the requirements of the American National Standard for Information Sciences—Permanence of Paper for Printed Library Materials, ANSI Z39.48-1984.

Copyright © 2015 Gwendolyn Zepeda
Printed in the United States of America

15 16 17 18 19 20 21 10 9 8 7 6 5 4 3 2 1

Contents

Zombies and the Bitten

Animals and Nature

For you.

Oh, to live on Sugar Mountain
With the barkers and the colored balloons,
You can't be twenty on Sugar Mountain
Though you're thinking that
You're leaving there too soon.
You're leaving there too soon.

—Neil Young

Addicts and Obsessions

Cocktail Hours

What if all my nights were Christmas lights on patios with tinkling drinks and fun conversations, sophisticated joshing with confident women and amusing men and the weather's nice and the mood is right and it lasts half the night and the next morning, I'm not sorry. I just drink coffee and relive the moments from the bar before. Anticipate the next night out.

What if so many bright nights made my weekdays feel heavier by comparison. Like a boat with all the ballast on the one side. An air balloon that's getting dragged down.

Dragged down. I get dragged on. And how do I escape? I'm tempted toward crime, I buy lottery tickets. I fill with resentment.

Until I tip. I let my boat get tipsy. It tilts this extra ballast into the darkening sea, the rising waves.

The Woman Who Taught Me to Smoke

The more we talked and drank, the better she felt about passing me the wand she'd filled with fire and vapor, the flavor she'd mixed by hand after months of careful consideration.

We smoked and drank and I didn't remember. We drank Prosecco in plastic cups. We celebrated something with mutual acquaintances and whispered like real-life friends.

Weeks later in my real life, I underwent stress and then thought about that vapor. Remembered that flavor and fantasized that it would fix my problem. Remembered her name with suspicion. A pusher, a dealer.

Weeks later in real life another of the party guests called and reminded me of videos I'd made while drinking that night. All funny, all charming, all emailed to mutual acquaintances, except for the one in which my smoker was crying, she said. Foreground or background unspecified.

Try as I might I can't guess what I'd been hoping to retain when I'd pressed Record.

I will never watch those videos. They're only for the women who didn't get invited, flat renderings of feelings they weren't asked to share. When I feel stressed, I imagine a taste like maple plus American Tobacco Number Three. I relive her sitting beside me at night. She's passing the fire wand. I can't see her face.

JFK

We love JFK. I wonder, though, what else there is to know about the man or his death? The men behind the death? The men behind those men? The grass on the knoll that was under their feet. The Texas live oak that shaded the shots above. Any flower that scented the air. The printed flowers on any of Jackie's dresses.

It's all been done, been said. Why chew the fat, the grass, the leaves, the clues again?

Masticate JFK. Masturbate the memory. Flog it. Fog it. The lesson learned by rote. And after, nothing known.

Calling

She's attracted to the prettiest ones
the most dramatic, the mugging-est, pouty-ful
Calling all hands to deck like
the sirens on rocks
all sparkle and screeches

She sees them as temptations.
Needs them.

But I feel them like suction
like undercurrents, toilets
sucking and flushing you down
They're forces to run from, I'm
permanently lashed to the mast

She's Odysseus and I'm a thousand
ears to hear his wailing.

Your Type

She has dark hair and eyes like a predator cat.
Seems to be petite in this picture, but round.
And her last name ends with A.

I have dark hair, round eyes like a rabbit.
Tall legs, not much like her,
my last name ends with A.

The Spaniards rode ships to the island of her people.
Liked what they saw and so took it. Left her slightly
lighter skin, a different kind of nose, a last name that
ends with an A.

The Spaniards found my people near the mountains.
Thought *how sexy*. Gifted them with baby ponies.
Read them poems. Fed them candy and wine.
Got sex. In exchange, I hope.
I hope they fell in love or had, at least, a
mutually agreeable transaction.
I got the lightest olive skin, this round nose, and my
last name ends with A.

You show me her picture, then leer at me. You
smile or smirk as you tell me predilections.
But I don't know why you think I care.
Your grandfather got here in another man's boat.
You've nothing I want and you're nothing
like the centaur.

Unspecified Design Anxiety

What if the mark you left turns out to be the wrong one
made so by wrong lighting fixtures, wrong shades of blue
if life was not art like you told yourself.
It was instead of money.
And nobody passes your pictures around
to imitate when it's over.

Her Trendy Shoes

The shoes she wore
don't know if they meant to be sexy
I think she meant cute
with the orange and the woven big platforms
ironic like baskets or
tapestries, beach blankets under her feet.

A basket, a blanket, a
tapestry under a woman
that holds her up, carries,
suspends her above dirty ground
presents her to you on a platform, a
stage or it may as well be like a genie
delivered this wish to you
on magic carpets that
fly here in tandem, a pair.

Anxiety Attack

When you explain that this feeling is only adrenaline
caused by glucose or lack thereof in my blood,
I can talk myself down. I can concentrate on fruits
or agave or aspartame substitutes. Think about the
things I control, then ignore all this trembling,
this stomach cramp, teeth grit, eye burn, bile,
this dread of the given situation. I can be
more machine-like. Create a fuel efficiency that
keeps me safe and makes my thoughts not matter.

The Ringmaster's Daughter

This is the kitten of the lion who bit you. I suckle him at my breast.

You raised me in a three-ring circus, master, surrounded by clowns and crowds. Controlled your lions in cages until it was time to let them out. Performed for the masses. And me, your apprentice? I learned that balancing act.

This is the kitten of the lion who bit you. I hold him on my lap.

I live in a house by the ocean. I lie under palm leaves and listen to the sea. No colors but blue-grays. No balancing tricks on the waves—I just breathe and they hold me.

This is the kitten of the lion who took you and maybe, someday, he'll grow up to bite me.

But I won't fall to the roar of the crowd in the tent where you called yourself master. No, I'd fall to the roar of the waves where I chose to make my home.

Monsters and Warriors

When Hansel and Gretel Grew Up

They moved out of the forest.
Gretel gave birth and got married.
Lives on a farm, sells pies on the side.
People think she's boring. The
same brown blouse and she
never lets her kids play outside
after dark. And she never drinks mead.

When Hansel and Gretel grew up, they
lost touch somewhat. Only the infrequent
letters when the tinker could carry them.
When paper to spare and the
candles burned long.

Her letters get melancholy. His get angry.
What happens when you come through a
messed-up thing like that together? Well,
only they know.

Their dad died and Hansel went back to the
forest to see about the cottage. Ended up
staying despite his intentions. His letters got
angrier. Gretel understood.

Gretel went up there to visit her brother.
Years since she'd been there and kids now
beside her . . .
She recognized the sour smell of mead.

Dim lights, distant rattles. That particular shape
to the bones in the trash piles. That look in
his eyes.

The look in his eyes now. She recognized.
It turned out she'd never understood.

Testimony

I was scared of a thing that might have happened. In daytime, I'm sure it never did.

At night, I don't trust daylit memories or instincts. In nightmares, like filmstrips, the feared thing occurs.

I've asked for witnesses, for plaintiff or defense. Strong boys say I shouldn't ever worry.

But I trust in my fears. Am willing to face things, admit them, tear open, suck clean, and thus cure.

Landscaping

I like mowing the lawn, especially in the mornings. It was 75 degrees with a nice little breeze to keep my hair off my neck. The handle of the mower vibrates fiercely and makes my hands numb, but it's not a completely unpleasant sensation. Little chunks of grass and ant hills fly up and hit my arms and legs, making them sting and making it sweeter, later, when I take my shower. I always start by mowing squares, to be more efficient. But my shapes change, eventually, for the flowerbeds and shrubs and things. All the shapes are pleasing. There goes a triangle of grass! There's another rhombus done! As I make decreasing hexagons around a crepe myrtle, I hear it plead *don't hurt me.*
I would never hurt you, baby. You know that.

Sometimes I mow in the evenings, instead, staying out until it's too dark to see. Farther and farther away I go, the noise not-unpleasantly numbing my mind. The weariness starts to drag at me, but maybe I can keep on pushing forever.

Eventually, I do hear my name bellowed angrily across the land. So I stop whispering promises to flora.

It's Friday Night

The ghosts who routinely arrive at one AM, when you're awake alone at night and your mind is overwrought from its concerns

Sometimes they start in the corners of your eyes, in the corners of the windows

Othertimes they lurk in the low-res photos online of women who allegedly wait for you because they know you're alone

No Title

The bravest thing is
daring to think
That the devils won't follow you anymore.
Those omens were wrong and
the unsaid prophecy untrue.
To think that you might not be

a dog in a yard
dumb drooling and flea bit,
blocked by fences that
no one else can see.

Maggots

Maggots stink in trashcans. Bend against/across the floor and terrorize bare feet. Portend bad things: The bad life passed, more bad to come.

Maggots grow into flies and eventually die as hardened iridescent shells in sun.

When you stop squealing and consider, you'll realize their temporariness. A very short segment of being. This didn't last. It can't. So get up. Fly away.

TV Bonding Time

It's good to watch cop shows with your kids. Every week, you'll tick off the plotlines on lists you keep in your mind. Sort them into:

- Bad things you've already told them about
- Bad things you need to explain
- Bad things avoidable with the right preparation

There's another list you keep in mind:
Bad things that happened to you.

Your kid hears your breathing. Notes plotlines that make you stay silent. Perceives more than you think and absorbs your lessons unsaid.

Carnie

He told me to sit on a certain horse. Said it went higher or faster than the ones fixed alongside. I was young enough to want to ride the carousel. Young enough to be polite.

It ended in the dark, my steed between the freeway and the bulk of machinery that hid me from my waiting aunt. He came around to bring me down.

When I told my aunt what happened, later, she only nodded. Unsurprised.

He said, "let me help you, miss," hot hand near my thigh. And I was old enough to recognize he wasn't yet skilled at taking things. Old enough to scare him with my eyes.

Portent

I was baking a cake to take to my mother-in-law's house for
Thanksgiving.
I'd bought raisins in an off-brand box. Opened the box, dumped
it over the batter.
I saw gnat-like creatures in the air. I looked into the box and it was
full of little worms.

I screamed and threw the box onto the floor. Cried because
I really hate worms and 'cause
I'd wanted this cake to
impress my mother-in-law.

He came into the kitchen and yelled, "What the hell?"
He looked in the bowl, said, "That shit won't kill anybody."
He stuck his hand in the batter, scooped out the worms and
chucked them in the trash.

I finished up the cake and watched my in-laws eat it later
but
I couldn't eat dessert myself, of course. And now
I only buy the raisins people say are full of pesticides.

We got divorced, too.
Mmm, mmm, good.

Dream Dictionary

They say the symbols of your dream must be particular to you.
They say only you can know their meanings.
And so I meditate.

The kittens that cry sound like They do, but then
tug at my womb like everything.

The woman that left (like She did) looked mean but when
breathed, smelled like freedom.

The monsters that made me scream in the dream, I
realize now, had your faces.

I'm screaming at your faces but I can't run away.

Texture

What is the texture of kindness,
preferred by the nice
with no unpleasant undertones, gross connotations?
Kitten fur on live kittens only?
Hydrated petals of uncut blooms?
Bland as the skin on the cheek of the loved one.

I like suede, sanded wood, crushed stones, skins of rabbits.
Something pilfered or ruined for
Me, for me, for me.

New Teeth

i.

Today at the dentist, I was in for a treat. My dentist is rather OCD and wanted to make sure my new fake teeth matched the others. So he brought in the lab tech, a man named Leon, who'd made my new canine and incisor. They clicked these caps into place and Leon looked. In office light, then sunlight from the window. Leon said we needed more violet. Took a tiny palette and painted right into my mouth. Clicked the caps off and baked them in the oven while I waited, while I lay on the dental chaise lounge and looked out the window. Thought about the job of making teeth. Thought about the man who makes them and knows, like an artist, that there's no such thing as white. His palette a rainbow of pastels. His mind a gallery of enamel, no doubt. A painter of crowns and a sculptor of them, too. I wondered if he'd gone to art school but didn't get to ask because

I didn't get to talk. Because I lay there as a canvas. A canvas that can hear its artists working. I guess you could say I was an object, but it felt okay. An object in a comfortable chaise lounge. I've had a lot of dental work because I have weak teeth. So I know what it means to submit. But I never take the laughing gas. I submit of my own volition as long as I can always reach out, grab the wrist. Kick the tools down, the power off. Throw down the bloody bib and leave.

I don't. I lie there. Force myself to release the tension from jaw and shoulder, and toe by toe. Allow the artists to do their art. Then Leon leaves and the drill starts. No more paint and no more ceramics. It's only the metalwork and ice sculpture now. Noise of chainsaws. Cold vibrations on my teeth, up my nose, and down to my toe by toe.

ii.

The longer I lie, the more I remember the times before. The time this dentist pulled that tooth from my head. And it had calcified, fused itself to my jawbone like a fossil. Like sta-lagmite or –lactite. Like when we were kids and the old clouded ice built castles in our freezers. Which our parents could defrost, with time and warm air, whereas my dentist could do no such thing with the tooth fused hard in my head. He could only shoot me with numbness, lever against my skull and pull. He pulled and pulled. Sweat made his forearms shine, eventually rolled on his temples. I felt like a monster—misshapen and shamed. He was the Beowulf to Grendel my mouth. Eventually, he won. Was exhausted and I didn't know how to comfort him. So I went home and fell asleep. Expected to have nightmares.

This time isn't as bad as that, or as bad as the other, with the blue gunk that rolled against my tonsils, so it seemed. The time with the screaming drill. The time the need for extra shots was revealed in bloody sharpness.

This time is barely anything. Or maybe I get used to it.

It goes so long, I run my mind-tongue over old thoughts like backs of incisors. The episode of Seinfeld where Jerry's dentist raped him, making fun of old fears. Steve Martin in that little shop of horrors, inexplicable dentist among monster plants. The "interesting fact" that dentists commit suicide more than any other day job. Idle musings, none of which match the moment.

iii.

The dentist is related to me (in law). A certain financial part of this is a favor. Which makes me wonder about his motivations. Of course he does it for family. Of course he does it because he's a Good Guy, like Beowulf. But what else? What complexities?

Does he believe that a woman's worth is her beauty, her smile makes her palate-able, so to speak? And is it a favor to his brother when he improves upon his brother's wife?

Does he believe that a human's worth is her beauty? That people should be the best they can, that he can help and so has the duty to do so, and especially for family first?

Does he believe that a tooth's worth is in its beauty? Can a tooth be simultaneously perfect and yet unique to its user, and can he be the one to make it that way?

Maybe he feels each of these things, each one embedded in, inseparable from the other.

I feel close to him, and not just because all his fingers are jammed into my mouth. But that was the beginning of it. I will move my tongue out of the way. I will not bite down. I will hold this position in silence, in appreciation.

Zombies and the Bitten

Five O'Clock

"Go home, lady" they say.
She's worked hard all day and now
it's time for others to celebrate
drink and brag, to
brush up against each other's
stiff bravado and grin the
jizz-seeped grins. To slap
each other on the backs
like hunting dogs and say
"Go home now, lady."

Her neck's hot as she goes.
Behind her eyes, the scenes
are red and wasps buzz in
her ears, her steps are muggy
and as she goes, she goes in the
wrong direction. And before
she's gone, she leaves
the others a slice of pie.
She wraps it slow and
careful and no one cares.

Conform

Sometimes I feel less than girly because I don't care about celebrities' personal lives.
Sometimes I feel guilty and try.

Flip through a magazine, find a picture of Darryl Hannah. I liked her in Blade Runner. She also played a mermaid once. She's tall. I wonder if she sometimes buys men's shoes, like I do. If she buys men's loafers.

I read somewhere she was smart. Read she was shy. Was she really shy or did she save her conversation for the other smart kids? Who reported this about her—the person who, in high school, chattered endlessly with groups of girls at a table in the middle of the cafeteria?

In this photo she's not wearing makeup. Not much. Does she like it that way? Does it hurt to have her hair curled, pulled, blown straight, teased higher? Or does she maybe like the makeup—black eye rims, red lipstick—the same way that you might like a mask?

What does Darryl Hannah do after a long day of filming? Does she go home and lie on her couch? Does she ever feel guilty for not thinking thoughts about other women's hair?

Acted Upon

A paper doll is balanced on a very thin line
Depends on the windflow which way it might fall.

Nature show is playing on your family TV
Depends on the camera angle, cadence of the narrator's voice, which way your sympathies lie, with the lions or with the gazelles.

The paper doll is waiting on the razor wire
Ready to jump the direction you blow.

A fat man is sweating on his family couch, there under a piece of wrought iron on the wall. The iron's on the wall 'cause the fat man's wife bought it. She wanted one; she saw them in all her friends' houses. The man's fat is due to the buffets on Tuesdays and nachos on Sundays while rooting for home teams. The sweat is because he exerts himself yelling. He warms to his subject. He talks about black children choosing to stay in the ghetto. They're stubborn. They don't want good lives. It's obvious. Look at their pants.

A paper doll can't stand upright, you dummy. At most a gust of air might blow it to its "feet" for fractions of a second.

Sometimes I feel like I have no choice.
Your breath blows me up to my feet and then out of this room.
I land on a savannah. Grow four legs, am running free.

And when you chase me, I turn around. Look you between the eyes and laugh at your nature.

Girl Cousin

This girl was bad. They told her so.
I eavesdropped and learned all
the ways of it.

They called her loud-mouthed.
She talks too much and
no one likes that. No man.
Hush her mouth.

I peeked but never saw her
alone, despite
the big mouth,
the bad slut,
the men bucked.

To the Man Who Failed to Sing "Boogie On, Reggae Woman" at Spotlight Karaoke

Any other drunken white guy would have given up—just pumped his fists and screamed his friends' names into the mic. But after seconds of forgotten-word terror, you kicked off your sandals and turned to face away from us. Compressed your body, rotated elbows and ass in tight rhythm. A dance we didn't need to see. A dance you couldn't help but do.

You were like a muttering salmon swimming upstream. No—a freaking melted glacier coming down the mountain's side. We watched you, all hearts syncopated, all our bottom lips bitten.

Boogie on, drunken white guy. You never leave my mind.

The Waiting Room of a Boring Place

When you're waiting in a beige place. Except for the lit-up box of colors that are candy. Sugar-filled tin cans all packaged in fancy fonts. Framed in bright glass, framed again by smooth buttons with numbers and letters you know. That call to you.

When you're told not to whine. Reminded of the covenant you don't remember making. Your every transmission deemed sub-par behavior by a man who is bored here. The man who brought you here and regrets his choices.

When you're older . . . How will you handle temptation? Will you know how to sublimate desire? If so, will you make it a habit? If not, will you act like your acts have no meanings? Hang out in night clubs, take all the drugs under fast-spinning neon. Or don't.

Will you hear your own transmissions? Will you turn in anger? Regret? When you're stuck in a boring place and hear a child whining near bright shining vending machines. Will you remember?

The Failed Initiation

You asked if I belong to your tribe.
You showed me your stockpiles of
stones, fallen feathers.
You waved your hand across a
vista. Told me, "This is ours."

You asked if I'd belong to your tribe.
You told me you knew your tribe was the
best and you'd say so as often as needed.

You told me to stay with your tribe.
You said that I seemed different today.
You said that you were lonely.

You told me you loved me and asked if I loved you.
I don't even know you. You have no way of knowing me.

Drag

I look like a boy in drag today. You know how drag queens will walk around their apartments in their robes, not yet dressed or wigged for the evening and yet not able to go without makeup, even in their own homes? That's how I looked just now when I saw myself in the restroom mirror here at work, with my short hair and the lip-colored lipstick the department-store beautician talked me into buying. All I need is a cigarette and a glass of clear liquor on the rocks.

Maybe I am a boy in drag. Especially here, where I don't feel like everybody else. I don't want to be the best secretary, or even the prettiest one.

I say a boy and not a man because this place is full of men. I don't share their raging urge to compete, to rake in the deals, to fuck all the women.

But I do want to impress you. If I knew some sort of dangerous sport, I'd do it in the freight elevator right now. A stunt to make you gasp, laugh, and clap your hands. But I don't know how. Plus I'm wearing these impediments—a skirt and high heels.

How about we meet near the freight elevator and I kiss you? Or do a sport with my eyelashes that makes you kiss me? And we stifle a gasp, giggle, then sigh. Come out to each other as rebels. Admit we're clever enough to hate everyone here. Declare that we don't care if we get fired for screwing around in the freight elevator. We're daredevils. Bitter clowns. Stuntmen and tough guys. And they're lucky we're not in the mood to kick ass.

But I'm wearing this dress for a reason.

They fired you. Then looked at my skirt and said, "Where's the pretty girl? Where's that girl who used to smile?"

And I said, "Here I am." Smiled for them. Touched up my make-up, flounced back to my place. Life costs money so I can't get fired. I dress up, I wig up, I smile.

Only I know I'm a boy in drag. And you knew, too. We're the same and I love you.

Or everyone here knows and they're clever enough to hate us.

Fat Guy

Big boy with the loud ice-jiggling Big Gulp.
Cords rubbing, feet scuffing.
Face sweats, breath drags.
We hear his heart struggle, hear his joints grind together like seeds in a grandma's *molcajete*.
Less-fat boys say "motherfucker better not die here."
Not clog clean carpets that stretch between cubes.
Skinny CEO makes faces and checks on the premiums, the company-pay portions.
Cuts down his own portions. Reminder to run.

Babies Wearing Skinny Jeans

Babies wearing skinny jeans
And do they think they're sexy?
And now you look offended when
you look at me but
all I hear is
Courtney, baby, you're so pretty
Madison, you look so cute
And look at little Averly she's gonna
break some hearts.
Babies wearing skinny jeans and
do they think they're sexy when they
look at you
You look at them and
all they hear is
what you said

Be a Girl

Don't resist that girly shit.
Coat your things in pink and
make your eyes like glossy stars.

Don't deride your frilly thoughts. Cry
vats over hurt puppies, minor
chords or disappointing men.

Avoid unhappy hags who want
their own damaged dollies, will
rip your hair and hold too tight.

Scratch like your familiar would. Reach inside and show your boiling
blood. And scream the octaves over.

The Infatuation Has Ended

I loved you as a tragedy. Made love because you needed me to. Unbeknownst. Cured you bit by bit with every touch and every grind. Felt like a nurse or a nasty benevolent angel. Selfless and kind even while I got off.

I lost you in reality. Saw you walking around in real life, making the choices you do. Wear a dumb sweater, date a dumb girl, paint yourself into that kind of life. Marry yourself to unhappiness. Earn an annual salary. Walk around with the saddest eyes, glistening enough to attract the angels.

I'm raging at your realness. Watching with dry eyes the choices you made and maybe I'm the dumbest one. I'm mad at your fall from mythological import. The time lost during those moments with you and those others in my imagination. The guilt, the shame I feel for my mistakenness. The slow-cooked ministrations for your so unworthy cause.

But you're not trapped in this veal pen. Your gate swings open and you have hands, not the blunt hooves, soft fur of a baby. So why don't you leave? And why do I walk by and check the gate?

I grieve for my nurse cap, my pretty white wings.

I Eat Crazy People

The rabbit smells the lion's shit and that which it has digested.
Discovers it's had antelope for lunch and
so can't possibly be hungry again.

The rabbit eats clover in the shadow of the lion,
enjoys the way his shade keeps others at bay.

As the rabbit dies,
is eaten,
she takes one bite of the lion in return.
Does she infect him with her spit, maybe?
The possibility makes her smile, right before it's over.

Janis

i.

My mom called from the institution where she lives. Something had jarred her and she needed to fret about the usual things, of course, but also to reassess the tragedies and mistakes of her past. I was home early and alone for once, so I listened to her longer than I normally would.

Every time I listen to my mom, she's a little bit different, or a lot different, depending on the kind of drugs she's on, or her point on a given drug's waxing/waning usefulness. She goes from disconnected to lucid, from panicky to ambivalent, from grounded in reality to very far above it. Always different, but never well.

This evening's monologue was nostalgic, yet paranoid as ever. She said she was glad I never got into trouble like my brothers, that I was always good and strong. She wished she could afford to send me $50 a month. She was sad about being so old and fat and ugly. She told me bad dreams about jealous ex-friends she believed had done her wrong.

She told me a story about something very bad from a long time ago. Two hippies got into a car with me and my brothers, alone in the park. Meanwhile, she did something with another hippie or two. She didn't want to do it, but she'd hoped they'd give her money so she could buy us things we'd cried for at the thrift shop that day. "You don't remember that day," she said.

I could have said, "I do remember. I've had nightmares about those men in that car for years, and now I know why." But I didn't say anything because she felt bad enough already. That was the day my dad took us away from her, she said. I don't remember that. "Losing y'all made me go crazy," she said. But that wasn't the truth.

She said the devil had possessed her that day and on several occasions before that. She said she'd been marked as a child, that some people were marked and that, all the time, she sees those who've been possessed.

I asked, "What would you do if the devil came to you now?"

She said, "That's a good question, Precious." She thanked God I was born unmarked and would never be possessed by the devil, unlike her. She'd think about what to do if he tried to get into her again. She gave thanks for my goodness and preciousness, and thanked God my father and his family were all pure immaculate conceptions, unlike her family, who were Nazis marked by the devil. She said to stick with my Chinese friends, because they'd help me make my car payments.

"I can make my own car payments," I said. And I didn't have any Chinese friends. But she's right when she says the devil won't possess me. I think she needs a game plan for the next time he comes to visit.

She started to tell me about the sheik she knew who wanted to marry me, if I'd agree to work in his restaurant. But I had to get off the phone.

ii.

My mom called yesterday. She was down because age is catching up with her and she looks "like she could be a grandma now." (I have three kids, making her a grandmother of 10 years.)

She said my dad wouldn't want her to move in again, now that she's so old and ugly. She sighed that she was unable to get boyfriends anymore, because of her face.

I asked her what she'd do if she were in an accident and lost her limbs, or had her face burned off in a fire. I asked if, after that, she'd still be a person worth knowing. And, if so, why.

"Thank you, Precious, for trying to cheer up your old, ugly mother," she said forlornly.

iii.

Things I think are crazy:

1. Worrying about your looks
2. Worrying about what some man thinks of you
3. Trading sex for anything
4. Worrying about the devil, Nazis, evil coke dealers, sheiks in Arabia, etc.

Sometimes I act crazy. I admit it.

iv.

I only have one good memory about her.

She used to let me play her guitar. I'd strum atonally and improvise songs. The songs were always about horses.

My mom would clap enthusiastically after each one. "That's so good, Precious! Mommy's so proud of you!"

Animals and Nature

Neigh

You thought I was a horse and so I might've.
You pictured saddle, then yourself, astride.
You likened windy tresses,
rounded quarters to those parts of me.
Imagined taming, breaking, riding.
Metaphors that applied.

I might be like a horse but not the
ride that you've been thinking.
I feel wind in my hair, my heavy quarters coming round.
You might cut off my hands somehow and
leave me hooves that thunder down. Pound blood
into mud in a vicious pudding.
Teeth that reach too far. A hearty scream.

Yesterday at Target

It's the day after Christmas so shoppers are perusing the fifty-percent-off decorations. A little boy accompanies his mother. She points to the word PEACE in gold plastic.

In Spanish, she asks her son, "What does that say?" In English, he tells her "Peace." In Spanish, she asks him, "What does that mean?" In English, he says loudly, "PEACE." She asks him again. He smirks and does a slight shrug with his hands, at me or at the invisible camera that must be taking in the scene.

I wanted to tell the woman, *"dice Paz,"* so she would know. But then she'd know I'd understood their conversation. Seen her son's disrespect. Guessed that he calls himself a different name at school—a distortion of his real name that's a word she can't pronounce.

She'd wonder if I could see her son struggling away from her arms. She'd wonder from my accent, maybe, if my father was somewhere sighing.

Dog Walk

Beast on a leash rains
destruction on a
galaxy of ants.
My hand on the
leash makes me
like a sort of
god, maybe.
Unmoved. Uncaring.
Only vaguely directing the
wave of misfortune.

Toxic Mold

There's the girl who lives there.
The mold doesn't bother her.
It won't until fifteen years away
and then she'll have allergies.
Reasons to host the Thanksgiving,
herself, or to
skip it altogether.

You know you've succeeded when you no longer tolerate.
When your body rejects what you breathed as a child.

A Fall

I felt my foot hit wrong on the stair
my weight pitch too far forward of center.
Corrected course but not enough.
A little too late.
I felt my wrist wrench, gripping
the banister.
Ankle bone ground on the edge.
Hip took the weight of far too much of me.
Carpet burns everywhere.
Carpet burns everything.
I heard my own scream
like a scared, angry goat.
I bleated. I called out the
pain, the rage, the regret
of my miscalculation.

A Broom Is a Broom

What they mean by elbow grease is the propensity to use the tools you're given. That's why all my brooms, whether plastic or straw, flattened out or beveled edge, are prone to daydream, leave the work half undone while imagining the future. Better worlds to brush with tender strokes and not this rush.

My broom's unfocused on the task and I refuse to buy a new one. My elbows stay clean but can drop a moist tear if someone criticizes dirt I've left behind. And I might feel bad when I get elsewhere.

The Other Artist

While we drank cheap beer in the sun he threatened
to make a 3D replica of my head, my face, the
exact shade of my lipstick and stick it to one of those
pony figurines with Pegasus wings or a unicorn
horn, my choice. Knowing his skills, I cringed.

I all-of-a-sudden knew
why my cousin had asked me, more than once,
"Are you going to write about our family again?"
The look in her eyes, even after I assured her I'd
do so with utmost attention to detail. Sad yet
funny with my own judicial edits.
The look in her eyes when she read what I'd
Already written. It's not that she could
say I was a liar.

And I told the artist no. And he asked why. He said,
"Don't you want to know what you look like
to me?" No. I felt then a fear of the one
who works to see a thing. Feared the
person who renders, at will, what he sees.

any situation at top speed. And sometimes
leaving makes the people left behind
call you names. They say "Bitch. She thinks she's too
good." But my ears are also heroic and turn the
opposite of supersonic.
Can fold against my head so I don't hear. They
fold down like my heart, which contracts to a
wad of steel.

In Elementary School, We Clapped Our Hands in Rhythm and Taught Each Other Shocking Words

[to be chanted to "Apples on a Stick"]

Pictures of a dick
they make me sick, then
I take out my own camera lickety split
Not because I'm dirty
Not because I'm clean
But because I'm wearing the right brand of jeans

Hey, guys, how 'bout a fight?
Hey, old man now, how 'bout a fight?

Here comes a lady in a mini skirt.
She can wibble, she can wobble, she can do the splits
Got herself a job and I bet you're pissed

One, two, three, four
You slapped on your daughter and you called her a whore
Five, six, seven, eight
You slapped your son's face, said he'd better be straight

Boys go to family court to
pay more child support
Girls go to bars in
shoes like movie stars.

Autumn Poem

I lie and say Fall makes me happy with its new beginnings and red orange splendor
while terrorized and achy in the mornings, which get darker every week day
The feeling's called relief and what's bringing it are light bulbs, bright games on my cell phone screen,
warm voices of the DJs on the radio who keep me from driving astray, driving back home, or
coming to a standstill in the middle of the freeway and cowering in the dashboard lights and
crying for the sun. What's making this okay is thoughts of starchy foods and parties.
Kill a deer, set sticks on fire. The same mentality. Beat a drum, draw
spells on the walls. Chant cheery words loudly but we'll always be scared of this dark.

Knowing What's Right

release me
my lover is the sun
it's only he who
burdens me with
only weight of air
a burn unminded

let go and let me
flee from your
dark hold
volcanic moods
oppressed embrace
your weighted face

but I'll scrabble, scratch and
dig myself deeper

Berries

That man came and lectured us on arm size. On DNA and evolution. On the nature of his brain, which entitled him to leer at us and couldn't be considered rude.

We saw that he was colorblind. You pitied and fed him. Gave him some very choice berries—the best that we had.

He couldn't tell the difference. He didn't say thanks.

Flirt

You say I flirt too much. You
call me flirt. Wide eyes,
moving lashes, flashing smiles
were how I got taught to be
polite. My mentors pretty
women and my targets
stubborn men.

See what you want.
Say what you wish.

If I wanted you, my ears
would sound like roaring
trains of lions. My tongue would
taste like metal of a pencil's end,
or blood. My feet would ride
a wave to you, then bed.

I can't say how it'd look to you;
I've never seen me flirt.

After the Hurricane

We stood on the banks of
I-45 that had turned into
a river
with tops of flooded cars that seemed to
float along like lily pads.

Those of us with
cars still working had
spent the morning
tracing the shape we were
trapped in. Came
back like scouts to
share our findings.
Heights cut off from Montrose.
Bayous filled to brims and
beyond. Here Be
Alligator Gars.

Those of us caught on the
wrong sides of these bayous will
spend the night on the futon.
Those of us who host will
suddenly remember the jigsaw
puzzle—where it's stored and how
we sort its pieces, sit together in
concentration and tolerate the heat.

One of us wheeled out a
cart and sold
corn on a stick.
Soft butter, sour cream, flecks of
pulverized peppers.
Another of us wished that he'd
thought of it first. Resolved to sell
burgers next hurricane.

We milled around on
muddy grass. Held off heading
back to the canned goods and
borrowed beds. A few of us were
still in shock. But most were
laughing and chatting. Flirting with the
passersby. Or on the phone with
others of us. Making plans for
next time. Or next day. Or
points to be determined in
our future.

Sad Shock

A woman who worked in our building killed herself this morning.

I rode up the elevators and escalator with her yesterday morning. We talked and talked about I don't know what. In the ladies' room she fretted she was having a bad hair day. She always said that.

Every time I went to get water, I glanced through the glass doors. Like always, she sat there, serene and alone at her desk, complemented by the floral arrangement and the wall-length window. A refreshing change of scene.

Someone said she was crying yesterday afternoon in the ladies' room. I didn't see—can't imagine it.

I wished aloud—offered the hundred dollars in my savings for the chance to go back in a time machine to yesterday, to somehow know what she was thinking, and to somehow change her mind.

They put a white ribbon on the glass doors. The flowers are drooping. Everyone has red eyes.

Fluffy

Last night I dreamed of kittens. At least three, each better than the last. Starting off cute/tiny/fluffy, making me say "Aw!" and then progressively becoming cuter, tinier, and fluffier, until I was nearly in tears. Then they changed into something else. One became like a faceted glass moving sculpture of a kitten, reflecting cuteness with every step. Throughout each metamorphosis, they meowed at me softly and held my gaze with their blue or green eyes.

Wesley Parks

Wesley Parks, you called my cell phone at 4:41 AM the other day.
You called again at 4:42.
Used my voicemail to apologize to Rose, Kevin, and the others.
Sorry you'd been out so long and that maybe no one had told them.
You had a seizure, got knocked into a coma lasting more than a day.
You sounded sincerely apologetic, and maybe also afraid.

Wesley Parks, I called your cell phone today.
Your mother answered.
I asked for you and heard conversation in the background,
maybe you and your dad.

Your mom said you'd been in a coma.

I told her about your misdirected phone calls.
Told her about Rose, Kevin, and the others.
Your message that didn't get through.

Your mom said you'd been in a coma.

I told her my concerns about you and Rose and Kevin and the others.
Your voice apologetic.
Your message un-parlayed.
Your fears that were evident, had now become mine.

Your mom said you'd been in a coma.
She apologized for the bother.
Her voice got defensive, a little bit frosty.

I worried for quite some time after she hung up.

Animals

When I was a child the teachers asked us, if we had to be an animal, what kind of animal would we be? And I would always think I was a baby coyote. But I'd lie and say a kitten or a pony because.

Later I thought, yes, I might be like a cat. In response to that question, which I continued to periodically ask, once a week or, at the very most, once a night, right before I fell to sleep.

Later I felt more like a fish, with big dead eyes.

Later a cat again, but a really tired or old one.

Now I don't know. Haven't asked myself in years. Which makes sense—a baby coyote wouldn't.

Blue Eyeliner

Whenever a relationship ends I have to
search for blue eyeliner. In pencil form, at
Walgreens or Eckerds. Cheap but not slutty.
Not navy, not aqua or teal, but
bright blue, like the sailors saluting or
cocktails in swimming pools.
A color that says I don't need you.

Party Bears

Before I learned it was a metaphor for the stockmarket—a piece of art that rich couples used to put in the bedrooms of babies—this print of a painting of bears would scare me.

It accosted me in our office. A thousand bears dancing in the forest. The ones who aren't dancing are serving wine or cooking fish. Some are just standing there, watching the dancers and touching on each other. A big freaking forest bear rave, with bears in different colors. Black, white, brown.

Did my boss bring it in, from his collection of less-liked antiques? Or was it simply *there*, like a poltergeist in a ranch house that was built on an Indian burial ground?

The secretary who'd been there longest walked over to discover the cause of my distress. *Oh, that bugs you? I never even noticed it.*

What were they doing, I wanted to know. "What is this, some kind of cult? Why are there *so many* of them? And why are some of them *white*, like *polar bears*? And why is this one wearing an *apron*? Are all the other ones supposed to be *naked*?" The single art history course I'd taken at UT was no help here.

The oldest secretary considered my questions.
They're there to have sex. They're having sexual encounters. Look at those two—they're about to get it on.
I was shocked.

She asked which bear I'd be. Said *I'm that one.* She pointed at one of the dancing bears. *And you're that one.* She pointed at a white bear leering down at something unseen in the mob.

I said no, and I pointed to the most innocuous-looking brown bear I could find in the foreground. Then I drew myself up to a very straight posture and walked back to my prison of a desk.

Recipe for Fun

1. Go to a nice store and buy a $10 jar of salt scrub. I like the herbal scents. You might like fruit, olives, vanilla.
2. Put the salt scrub in a cabinet in your bathroom. Leave it there until it's ripe. You'll know it's ripe when you start screaming at people for really petty reasons and fantasizing aloud about quitting whatever it is you do.
3. Give everyone in your house pizza, cat food or video games until they aren't squealing at you anymore. Go into your bathroom and close the door.
4. Crouch down in your tub like a scared, naked animal with your jar of salt scrub. Open it up and stick your big fist in it and squish all the contents between your knuckles. Scoop out big handfuls of the salt and smear it all over yourself, stopping to rub it into your skin every so often. Especially your feet. Jeez, your feet are all dried up and rough. Do your back and your neck, too.
5. Pretend you're back in the womb. Unless, of course, your mom was a drug addict or something while she was pregnant with you. In that case, you have permission to pretend you're in my womb. I didn't smoke or drink when I was pregnant. I didn't even drink caffeine. I did yell at my husband a lot, though. I went into screaming, hormonally induced rages from time to time. But maybe that will make you a more assertive person. And, besides, it wasn't always like that. Most of the time I listened to really good music. You would have had good taste in music and a bit of artistic talent if you'd come out of me.
6. It's up to you if you want to salt one of your kids so he'll stop asking you if he can take a bubble bath.

7. Turn on the shower while you're still sitting on the floor of the tub. Let it wash over your head like the rain you're always trying to avoid in the outside world.
8. Before you try to get up, clean your palms and the soles of your feet really well with soap or maybe even with shampoo, because you'll be super slippery and you don't want to fall down. ("I feel like rubber," your kid might say. "I feel like a dolphin!")
9. Get up and take a regular shower.
10. Go back to life.

Ants

The other day I was working on a story. Every time I stopped working and went to the bathroom, there'd be a giant ant on the bathmat, standing there, waiting.

I don't know if the ants were trying to tell me that the story was fine the way it was, or that I should go ahead and take it in the direction I was envisioning. Or maybe they were there to be supportive and inspiring.

But, either way, I had to kill them all. I apologized profusely to each one before smashing it under the bath mat as hard and quickly as I could.

The Downstairs Colombian's Particular Insanity

He takes pride in the fact that he's Colombian,
not Mexican like all the other workers.
He used to live in France with two women. They'd have sex.
I know because he told me, one day while he
custom-made my salad.

He handed me my salad, said *Oh, but I don't even*
know your name.
I said *I know* and walked away.
And he looked sad and slightly bitter.
Oh, well. That's life, Philippe.

He used to hit on my coworker Lisa.
Went so far as to slip notes into her salad box.
She said they smelled like Hai Karate.
I don't have hard feelings. I still order salads for
lunch. But now Philippe, he calls me *preciosa*.

That word means "precious." But that's not what it
means. Here that's what you can call a child. What an
old Southern lady can call anyone. It's what my
parents used to call me, when I was a girl.

In Spanish, though, it's what you call your lover.
Not what you say to a stranger for whom you
occasionally make salads for money.

He whispers it to me when he hands me the food. Loud enough to hear. At the same time, quiet enough to deny. *You don't want onions. You don't like them, huh, preciosa?*

I imagine how angry it makes him to work here. With Mexicans. For white men. Unvalued. Not recognized. Make salads for women who do not express proper gratitude.

I stopped listening. Began to stop seeing him, after a while.

The Sad Monkeys

Monkeys want cell phones but get rebuffed.
It's a very sad story. Monkeys live at the zoo.
They see humans using cell phones. The
monkeys, then, want cell phones of their own.

Give the monkeys cell phones. Please.

But no. Instead, the keepers "train" the monkeys
not to want the cell phones anymore. They do this by
giving them old, broken cell phones, coated with
"sticky substances" the monkeys "don't like."

Give the monkeys cell phones! They *want* them.

The keepers say the monkeys are supposed to live
naturally, there in the zoo. No cell phones, no
people food thrown by the people that watch.
See the sign? See the popcorn, the corn dogs, the beer?

Give the monkeys cell phones and pre-program each of their
cell phones with the phone numbers of all the other monkeys.
Then let things evolve.

The Man Who's Sitting Next to Me in this Photograph

He had some jacked-up stuff happen in his life.
He was a sergeant in our Vietnam War.
People ask me where he was stationed and
what he did, and I don't really know because
he doesn't like to talk about it.

He used to play the saxophone, the flute, and the
recorder before the war. Now he doesn't.
He saw his best friend die.

He wasn't drafted. He says he volunteered so
people who really didn't want to go
wouldn't have to.

He's cynical in the wittiest way you can
imagine. He can pull philosophical themes from the
very worst TV shows and movies.

He knows how to read Tarot cards.
But he says they're not a game.
So don't ask.

Morning Game

When it was time to turn off the TV, we played TV. We played Woody Woodpecker, taking turns being its namesake. We played Price is Right, using cushions from the couch, stacked and offset to Create an aisle.

"Come on down!" we'd say to each other. "You're the next contestant on the Price is Right!"
Before you said that, you had to say the contestant's name. It occurred to me that I needed one. Not the name I'd learned to write in school—not "Gwendolyn Zepeda." That wasn't a contestant.

I announced myself, then. "Wendy Reynolds, come on down. You're the next contestant on the Price is Right!" Then we sang the music as I tripped down the cushion aisle. My brother cried until I also christened him. Said, "Zonky Reynolds, come on down!" because whoever heard of a contestant named Zonky alone, or Enrique Zepeda for that matter. He smiled as he ran off the couch, down the cushions, to the mattress where we slept and ate cereal and watched TV.

Aunt Sylvia

On Friday nights, when there was nothing else to do, she used to tell me, "Go get the keys from your daddy. Let's see the Freak Show."

She meant that we would cruise Westheimer near Montrose, where all the prostitutes, drag queens and pretty young boys walked the streets and sometimes climbed into the other cars.

Afterwards, we always went to Baskin Robbins, where she would watch me eat a banana split with the most eclectic combination of flavors my thirteen-year-old mind could contrive.

This was after her mother had died. After she'd babysat and cleaned up after her mother, who was busy tearing out of life in a hilariously awful rampage of dementia and incontinence.

This was before I'd become a real teenager and fought my way away, out of our house.

This was the quiet time for her, when she ventured out with me to see marvelous things. She carefully monitored my growth into someone who would go on to see more, later, without her.

Also by Gwendolyn Zepeda

Better With You Here

Falling in Love with Fellow Prisoners: Poems

Houston, We Have a Problema

Lone Star Legend

To the Last Man I Slept With and All the Jerks Just Like Him